Cold front
on a weather
map

Lightning
strikes a tall
building.

Mirage – a
reflection of
the sky on a
layer of hot air

Thunderclouds overhead

Leaf with dew

EYEWITNESS
EXPLORERS

Weather

Written by
JOHN FARNDON

DORLING KINDERSLEY, INC.
NEW YORK

A DORLING KINDERSLEY BOOK

Project editor Christine Webb **Art editors** Thomas Keenes, Carol Orbel
Senior editor Susan McKeever **Senior art editor** Jacquie Gulliver
Production Catherine Semark **U.S. editor** Charles A. Wills
Editorial consultant Ron Lobeck

First American edition of this Eyewitness™ Explorers book, 1992
10 9 8 7 6 5 4 3 2
Dorling Kindersley, Inc.,
232 Madison Avenue, New York, NY 10016

Copyright © 1992 Dorling Kindersley Ltd., London

Library of Congress Cataloging-in-Publication Data
Farndon, John.
Weather/ by John Farndon – 1st American ed.
p. cm. – (Eyewitness Explorers)
Includes index.
Summary: Discusses such elements of weather as clouds, wet air, frost, ice, wind, and air pressure.
Includes some projects.
ISBN 1-56458-019-9
ISBN 1-56458-020-2 (lib. bdg.)
1. Weather – Juvenile literature. 2. Weather forecasting – Juvenile literature.
[1. Weather] I. Title. II. Series.
QC981.3.F37 1992   91-58210
551.5 – dc20   CIP
                                                                             AC
Color reproduction by Colourscan, Singapore
Printed in Italy by A. Mondadori Editore, Verona

Contents

What is weather?

Weather is just the way the air around you changes all the time. It can be still, moving, hot, cold, wet, or dry. Most importantly, weather is the way water changes in the air. Without water, there would be no clouds, rain, snow, thunder, or fog. Weather plays a big part in our lives and affects many of the things that we do.

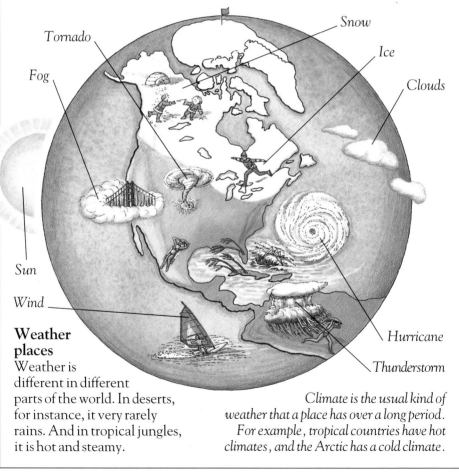

Tornado

Snow

Ice

Fog

Clouds

Sun

Wind

Weather places
Weather is different in different parts of the world. In deserts, for instance, it very rarely rains. And in tropical jungles, it is hot and steamy.

Hurricane

Thunderstorm

Climate is the usual kind of weather that a place has over a long period. For example, tropical countries have hot climates, and the Arctic has a cold climate.

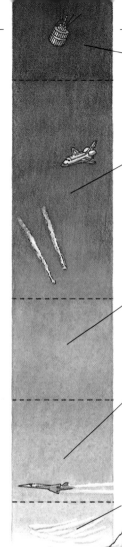

Satellites are stationed in the exosphere, 300 to 1,000 miles from Earth.

The thermosphere is from 50 to 300 miles from Earth. Here, you'll find the Northern and Southern lights, space shuttles, and meteorites.

The mesosphere is between 30 and 50 miles from Earth. Some of the ozone layer is found here.

The stratosphere is between 8 and 30 miles from Earth. The Concorde supersonic jet flies here.

All our weather happens in the troposphere.

Mighty puff

The ancient Greeks used to think that wind was the Earth breathing in and out. Now we know it is simply air on the move.

The atmosphere

Our planet is surrounded by a thin blanket of gases called the atmosphere. Weather happens only in the very lowest layer, the troposphere.

Weather forecasts

Weather experts can now use satellites to help them make more accurate forecasts. This satellite photograph helps to tell which way a storm is traveling.

The seasons

You can expect a certain kind of weather at certain times of the year. Winter days are often bitterly cold or stormy, while summer days may be warm and sunny. It all depends on the season. Some places have just two seasons, a wet one and a dry one. Other places have four: spring, summer, autumn, and winter.

Winter sleep
Many animals like mice sleep away the winter to save energy. This is called hibernation.

Heat makes far-off hills appear hazy.

Summer
The sun is high in the sky at noon, and days are long and warm. Hot weather may be broken by thunderstorms.

Spring
Once winter is over, the sun climbs higher in the sky, and the days get longer. Nights are cold but days can be warm.

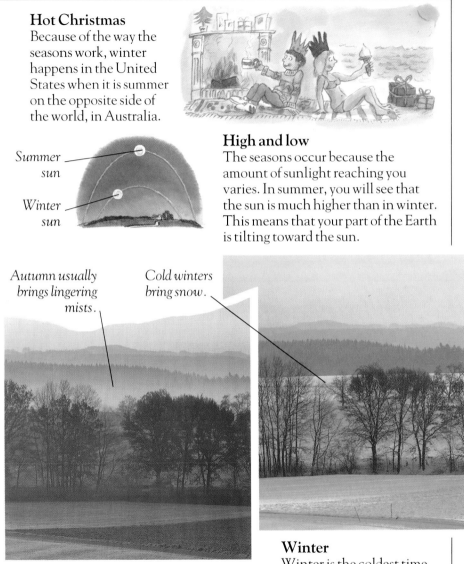

Hot Christmas
Because of the way the seasons work, winter happens in the United States when it is summer on the opposite side of the world, in Australia.

Summer sun

Winter sun

High and low
The seasons occur because the amount of sunlight reaching you varies. In summer, you will see that the sun is much higher than in winter. This means that your part of the Earth is tilting toward the sun.

Autumn usually brings lingering mists.

Cold winters bring snow.

Autumn
During autumn, the nights get longer and cooler again. Mornings are often misty. Sometimes they are frosty.

Winter
Winter is the coldest time of year. The days are so short and the sun hangs so low in the sky that the air barely warms up.

The three clouds

Clouds come in all kinds of shapes and sizes, but they are all made of billions of tiny water drops or even ice crystals floating in the sky. There are three basic types – fluffy white "cumulus" clouds, huge blankets of "stratus" clouds, and wispy "cirrus" clouds.

What makes a fluffy cloud?
Cumulus clouds are made when sunshine warms up bubbles of moist air and causes them to rise quickly. As they get higher, they swell and are cooled so that the moisture turns into a mist of water droplets.

Cumulus clouds are about 1,500 feet above you.

Cumulus clouds
Fluffy cumulus clouds are the clouds you usually see in good weather, when the sky is blue. They look like cotton balls and are always changing shape.

This cloud's fluffy shape shows how the bubbles of warm, moist air billow out.

Cirrus clouds

Feathery cirrus clouds form very high up in the sky. It is so cold up there that they are made not of water droplets, but of tiny ice crystals.

Cirrus clouds high up in the sky often signal bad weather.

Mare's tails

Cirrus clouds are often called mare's tails because strong winds high in the air blow them into wispy curls – just like the tail of a horse.

Stratus clouds build up when warm, moist air rides up slowly over a bank of colder air.

Stratus clouds

The word "stratus" means "layers" in Latin, but you rarely see the layers in a stratus cloud. You just see a huge gray sheet of low cloud that can stretch for hundreds of miles.

Cloud spotting

Clouds come in many shapes and sizes – some large and fluffy, some small and wispy. It all depends on whether they are formed from water droplets or ice crystals. Weather experts identify clouds by how high they are in the sky, and whether they are layered (stratus) or in heaps (cumulus).

Cirrostratus
Clouds that form very high in the sky always start with the word "cirro." Cirrostratus clouds are made of ice crystals.

Sometimes a colorful ring appears in cirrostratus or high altostratus clouds.

Altostratus
Medium-height clouds start with the word "alto." Altostratus is a layer of clouds made of water droplets.

Nimbostratus
These thick layers of cloud start near the ground and can be very tall. They can bring hours of rain or snow.

Stratus
Thick layers of stratus cloud hang close to the ground. Sometimes you can see the sun through it, looking like a silver disk.

Sketching clouds
A good way to get to know cloud shapes is to draw them. Keep sketches simple by drawing just the outlines and texture.

Cirrocumulus

These tiny balls of icy cloud often form what is called a "mackerel sky" because they look like the scales of a mackerel fish.

Cirrus

Cirrus tend to be the highest clouds of all. They form streaks across the sky that tell of strong winds blowing. They are a sign of changing weather.

The top of a cumulonimbus cloud looks like an icy wedge.

Altocumulus

These are medium-height cumulus clouds. They look like flattened balls of cotton that are almost joined together.

Cumulonimbus

These are the towering clouds that give us thunderstorms and tornadoes. A big one may be taller than Mount Everest!

Cumulus

Fluffy cumulus clouds are easy to spot. These low-level clouds sometimes develop during the day and get bigger, giving showers.

Stratocumulus

If you see long rolls of these medium-height clouds, they usually mean fair weather is on the way. They are made by cumulus clouds spreading out in layers.

Sometimes bolts of lightning flash from the base of the cloud.

Wet air

You might not know it, but you're sitting in a sea of water. Like a sponge, air soaks up invisible water vapor. All air contains water vapor, but how much it holds – the air's "humidity" – depends on how hot and dry it is where you are.

Dew wonder
If air cools down, it can hold less water. After a cool night, leaves and grass are often covered with drops of water, or dew, that the air could not hold.

High up, water vapor turns into drops of water. This is called condensation.

Wet breath
When you breathe out, you fill the air with water vapor. If the air is very cold, the vapor turns into millions of tiny water droplets and your breath looks "steamy."

1 Damp air
Water gets into the air because the sun heats up oceans and lakes. Millions of gallons of water then rise into the air as invisible water vapor. This is called evaporation.

Big clouds are so full of water that some falls to the ground as rain.

2 Falling rain

When some clouds get really big, the tiny droplets of water in them bump into one another and grow. Soon they are so big that they fall to the ground as rain. This is called precipitation.

Once they have lost some of their water as rain, clouds begin to vanish.

Rain is the same water going around and around in a never-ending circle called the water cycle.

3 Running away

Some rain falls straight into the sea. Rain falling on the ground fills up rivers and streams, which run back to the sea. And so the cycle can begin all over again.

Some rainwater seeps through the ground before reaching rivers.

Rain and drizzle

Without clouds, it wouldn't rain. Rain is simply drops of water falling from clouds filled with water. Clouds get full because drafts carry air up until it cools, and the water vapor turns into drops of water, which fall as rain. When the raindrops are very fine, they fall as drizzle.

Raining cats and frogs

Rain sometimes brings other things aside from water – such as maggots, fish, and even frogs!

This big hailstone has been cut in half.

See how the ice builds up in layers, like the layers of an onion.

Raining ice

Sometimes rain falls as solid chunks of ice called hailstones. These are made when raindrops are tossed high up in huge clouds and freeze into ice. As they are bounced up and down inside the cloud, they grow into big hailstones.

Deep end

The wettest place in the world is a mountain in Hawaii, where over 36 feet of rain falls every year.

Base of large gray thunder-cloud full of water

Large drops of rain falling as downpour

Rain approaching

This picture shows a heavy rainstorm over Arizona's Grand Canyon. Short, heavy showers like this are common in warm places because the warmth can make air rise rapidly to create big rain clouds.

Weather moos

According to some country folk, you know rain is on its way when cows are all lying down in a field.Unfortunately, the cows sometimes get it wrong!

Raindrops

Every cloud holds millions of water drops and ice crystals. They are so tiny that they are held up by air alone. Some big clouds have water drops at the bottom and ice crystals at the top. Before rain falls, the droplets grow much bigger. Some grow by bumping into one another and joining together. Others grow by condensation.

Tiny water droplets bump into one another and cling together as they fall.

See how they grow

When water drops grow by condensation, water vapor freezes onto ice crystals, and they grow into snowflakes. Then they fall from the cloud. As they fall through warmer air, they melt into raindrops.

Raindrop sends up a splash of water.

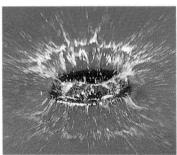

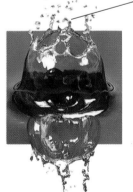

Drop by drop

As a raindrop falls, it gathers up smaller ones below, growing all the time. The biggest raindrops are about one-fifth of an inch across. Drizzle is less than half that size.

Drizzle does not make splashes on water.

Make a rain gauge

If you want to keep a record of how much rain falls,
why not make yourself a simple rain gauge like this?
You will need a large plastic soft-drink bottle, scissors,
tape, a heavy flowerpot, and a notepad and pencil.

*If necessary, use
masking tape to hold
the "funnel" in place.*

1 With an adult present, use a pair of
scissors to cut the neck off the bottle.
Turn the neck upside down and rest
it inside the bottle.

2 Stick thin strips of
tape 1 inch apart up
the side of the bottle.

*If the bottle is 5 inches
across, every half-
inch of water in the
bottle shows a half-
inch of rain.*

*Before you start, fill
the bottle with water
up to the first mark.*

3 Set your gauge outside in a heavy
flowerpot. Then every day, or week,
make a note of how much water there is
in the bottle, using the marks to help you.

4 Every time you measure
the water, you can plot the
result on a graph like this.

21

Fog and mist

On a clear day, you can see for miles if you are high enough. But at other times, the air may be so thick with fog that you can barely see across the road. Fog and mist look like smoke, but they are actually tiny drops of water floating in the air. In fact, fog is cloud that has formed at ground level.

Fog cuts visibility (the distance you can see) to less than 1,000 yards.

Souper fog
Dust and smoke make fog much worse. Before coal fires were banned in the 1950s, London had some of the world's worst fogs – called pea-soupers because they were so thick and green!

Night fog
It gets foggy when the air is too cool to hold all its moisture, or water vapor. At night, when the sky is clear, the ground gets cold. It cools the air close to it, making water droplets form in the air. The thickest fogs form when the air holds a lot of moisture.

Golden mist

San Francisco's Golden Gate Bridge is often wrapped in mist because the warm California air is chilled by cold sea currents.

Morning mists are often seen in valleys, where cold air collects during the night.

Morning mist

Mist is made in the same way as fog but is not as thick as fog. It clings close to the ground, and you can see over the top of it. Long, clear autumn nights often bring misty mornings – especially in valleys, because cold air drains down into a valley during the night.

Mist is thickest just above the ground, because it is the ground that cools the air.

Frost and ice

In winter, the days are short and the sun hangs low in the sky, so we barely feel its warming rays. On clear nights, there is no blanket of clouds to keep in even this warmth. Then it gets so cold that moisture in the air freezes, covering the ground with sparkling white frost.

Keeping the cold out
People used to say that frost was the icy touch of evil Jack Frost.

When moisture in the air freezes, it becomes frost.

Frosty fingers
Sometimes, plants get so cold that moisture in the air freezes on them instantly in spiky fingers. This is called hoarfrost.

Pretty cold!
If it is very cold, you may see lovely patterns of fern frost on your windows. This is made when tiny water drops on the glass turn into ice. As more moisture freezes on top of these icy drops, feathery fingers of frost begin to grow.

Rime frost looks like icing around the edge of petals.

All white

Frost coats the ground and plants with thousands of tiny ice crystals. This may happen because the ground is icy cold – especially on clear spring nights. Sometimes, though, a damp icy wind makes frosty bands form on the edge of flower petals and leaves. This is called rime frost.

Winter sports

It is lucky for us that ice floats on water. Even when it is really cold, ponds and lakes are covered with just a thin layer of ice. If ice sank, not only lakes but all the seas would slowly turn into solid ice!

👋 *Be careful! Never walk on water that is covered with ice.*

Ice is frozen water.

Snowy weather

High up where the air is below freezing (32°F), clouds are made up of tiny ice crystals. These crystals grow into large snowflakes, which drift downward and melt into rain if the air gets warmer. But if it is near or below freezing all the way down to the ground, we get snow instead.

Winter sports
Snowy, freezing weather can have its benefits! Skiing and tobogganing down a snow-covered slope are popular winter sports.

It snows the most when the temperature is at freezing point.

White blanket
Once snow has covered the ground, it may not melt for a while, because the white snow bounces away warming sunlight. If it melts and then refreezes, the crisp, frosty blanket will last even longer.

Snow wonder

Put some snowflakes on a colored surface and look carefully at them under a magnifying glass. You will see that they are all hexagons, which means they have six sides. But just as no two people are exactly the same, so no two snowflakes are identical.

Snowflakes look like delicate lace.

All snowflakes have six sides.

You'll have to work quickly before they melt!

"Wet" snow makes good snowballs.

Avalanche!

Snow can be destructive. When spring arrives, the snow on mountainsides starts to melt and may cause an avalanche. Tons of ice and snow crash down into the valley below, burying everything in their path.

Avalanches often happen in spring.

All sorts of snow

When it is below freezing, snow is powdery and "dry" and is useless for making snowballs! But when the temperature is just about freezing, snowflakes are large and the snow is "wet." It is easily crushed into heavy snowballs.

27

From breeze to gale

Winds are simply the air around us moving. Sometimes, the air moves so slowly that the wind is too weak to lift a feather. At other times, it moves so fast that trees and walls are blown down, and even cars may be swept into the air.

Clouds sweep across the sky.

Force 2: Light breeze

When a light breeze blows, the weather is usually clear. You can feel air on your face, hear leaves rustle, and see plumes of smoke gently drifting.

Small tree swaying

Force 5: Fresh breeze

During a fresh breeze, clouds often start to scud across the sky, and small trees sway. Crested waves form on lakes.

Wind force

In 1805, a British sea captain named Francis Beaufort began to measure winds by counting how many sails his ships could safely use. He divided winds into 13 "forces," from calm to hurricane. Later, his idea was adapted for use on land.

Wind power

Windmills were once used to grind grain. Now they are used to make electricity. Forests of windmills like these can make enough electricity to light a whole town.

Blown away

The world's windiest place is Antarctica, where winds blow at more than 60 mph!

Stormy sky

Force 7: Near gale

During a near gale, the sky may be dark and stormy. Large trees sway, and it becomes hard to walk against the wind.

Broken branch

Force 9: Strong gale

When the wind blows at strong gale force, the sky may be covered with thick clouds. Large branches snap, and chimneys can be blown off roofs.

Under pressure

You can't feel it, but the air is pushing hard on you all the time. This push is called air pressure. Sometimes pressure is high; sometimes it is low. Changes in air pressure bring changes in the weather and make winds blow.

Ups and downs

Changes in air pressure are measured on an instrument called a barometer. When pressure is low, the weather is often wet and cloudy. When it is high, the weather is usually dry and clear.

The barometer measures pressure in units called millibars.

When the air pressure drops, stormy weather is on the way.

When the air pressure stays high, the weather is likely to stay fine.

Jumbo force

On average, air presses with the same force as an elephant balancing on a desk! But rather than in elephants, air pressure is measured in millibars (mb). For example, 1050 mb is high pressure, and 900 mb is low pressure.

Make a barometer

This barometer will help you predict the weather. Make it on a rainy day when the air pressure is low, or it will not work. You will need a glass jar or straight-sided glass, a long-necked bottle, water mixed with food coloring, and a marker.

When the water is high in the bottle, pressure is high and it should stay fine.

When the water is low in the bottle, pressure is low and it will be stormy.

1 Set the bottle upside down in the jar so that it rests on the rim. The top of the bottle should not quite touch the bottom of the jar.

2 Take the bottle out and pour enough colored water into the jar so that it just covers the neck of the bottle when it is in place.

3 On the jar, mark the level of water in the bottle. Set your barometer in a place where the temperature is fairly constant. Mark any changes in the water level over the next few weeks.

Right windy

Because the world is spinning, winds spin too – out of high and into low pressure areas. Try standing with your back to the wind. If you live north of the equator, high pressure will be on your right. South of the equator, it will be on your left.

31

Superwinds

In summer, tropical places are hot and sunny. But during autumn, the skies darken and terrifying storms sweep in from the sea, bringing fierce winds and lashing rain. These storms are called hurricanes, typhoons, or cyclones, depending on where you live.

Picture of a hurricane taken from a satellite in space

An eye for a storm
A hurricane starts when hot tropical sunshine stirs up moist air over the sea. It then whirls over the ocean in a giant spinning wheel of cloud, wind, and rain.

Stormy people
Every hurricane is given a name. Once, only girls' names such as Jane and Diana were used, but now boys' names are used too.

Hurricane slice
What goes on inside a hurricane? Fierce winds hurtle around the bottom of the storm, but the center is dead calm. The air that spirals up around the center builds up tall rain clouds.

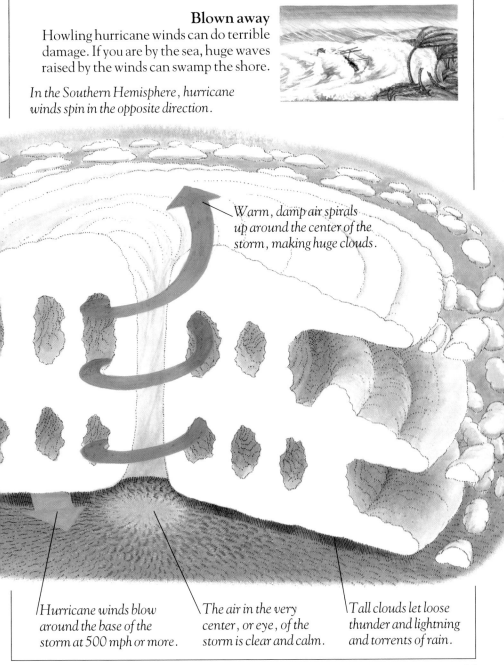

Blown away

Howling hurricane winds can do terrible damage. If you are by the sea, huge waves raised by the winds can swamp the shore.

In the Southern Hemisphere, hurricane winds spin in the opposite direction.

Warm, damp air spirals up around the center of the storm, making huge clouds.

Hurricane winds blow around the base of the storm at 500 mph or more.

The air in the very center, or eye, of the storm is clear and calm.

Tall clouds let loose thunder and lightning and torrents of rain.

33

Twisters

Tornadoes, or twisters, are whirling funnels of air. They hang down from thunderstorm clouds that form in very hot and humid weather. Twisters usually last about 15 minutes, but if the bottom of a funnel touches the ground, it will suck up and smash everything in its path instantly.

Twister alert
If you see thunderclouds with small, rounded "lumps" beneath them, they are a sign that a tornado is on the way. These bulging clouds are called mammatus.

Twisters are like the funnel that forms when water is sucked down a drain.

White column
Inside a tornado, air is sucked upward and starts to spin at enormous speed. This approaching tornado is white, because it has not yet touched the ground and picked up dust and debris. If the train is not in the tornado's path, it will be safe.

Waterspout

When a tornado develops over calm seas, it is called a waterspout. Mist, spray, and water are sucked up into the twisting funnel.

Tornadoes are most common in the United States.

Strange but true

Tornadoes have been known to whirl objects high up into the air and then set them down, completely undisturbed, nearby.

At the center of the tornado, wind speeds can reach 250 miles per hour. They are the fastest winds on Earth.

On target

As the bottom of the tornado touches the ground, it sucks the bridge, dust, debris, and train cars high into the sky. Then it hurls them back to the ground.

A tornado makes a deafening roar as it passes by.

35

Hot weather

In places where the sun sits high in the sky at midday, the days are long and the weather is hot. Hot weather often comes with high pressure areas, because they bring clear skies and light winds. High pressure can last for a long time, making hot, sunny weather last for days on end.

Mirage
Sometimes, on a very hot day, you may see a mirage – a pool of water on the road ahead. Then, as you approach, it disappears. What you are actually seeing is the reflection of the sky on a layer of hot air just above the ground.

Thermometer
Thermometers help us to measure the temperature. Sealed inside a glass tube is a silvery liquid metal called mercury. Mercury swells as the temperature rises and shrinks as it gets colder.

Glass tube holding mercury

The power of the sun
The sun gives off energy, which we feel as heat. Its energy can be trapped by solar panels and made into electricity. Solar-powered cars run on the sun's trapped energy.

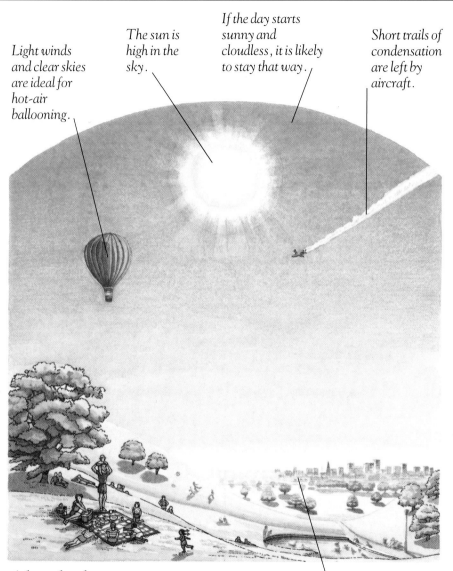

Light winds and clear skies are ideal for hot-air ballooning.

The sun is high in the sky.

If the day starts sunny and cloudless, it is likely to stay that way.

Short trails of condensation are left by aircraft.

A hot, dry day

On a hot day, there are no clouds in the sky because the air is dry and calm. Hot, humid weather is more unpleasant, because water vapor in the air makes us feel sticky and uncomfortable.

"Smog" is made when dust and pollution are trapped near ground level.

Dry weather

Some countries have plenty of water, and shortages are rare. But in many parts of the world, water is scarce and people can never be sure when it will rain next. Droughts happen when for months – or even years – on end, the Earth's surface loses more water than it collects. In some places, called deserts, rain almost never falls at all.

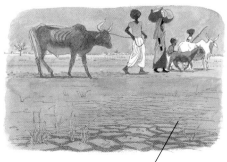

During a drought, the land becomes parched and cracked, and food crops die.

Drought

If droughts last for a very long time, animals die of thirst, crops wither in the hot sun, and people have to go without food – they may even die of starvation.

In true deserts, plants and animals can live only near oases, which are areas of open water.

Desert scene

You'll often find deserts inland, next to mountain ranges. The mountains act as a shield and keep rain-bearing clouds away. Semi-deserts like this one in Arizona have a little rainfall – enough to support plants that can store water, like cacti.

*Not all deserts are hot.
Central Antarctica is one
of the driest places on Earth.*

Dust bowl

Drought can affect many people's
lives. In the 1930s, the Great Plains
of North America suffered from a
disastrous drought that created a Dust
Bowl. Terrible dust storms buried
crops and houses, and many people
were forced to leave their homes.

*Large stones
at corners*

*Small pebbles
to weigh down
center*

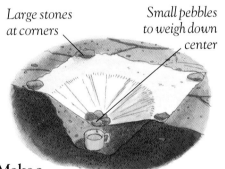

Death Valley

One of the driest and hottest
places in the world is Death
Valley in California. In the
past, people have died of
thirst in the extreme heat.

Make a
garden moisture trap

Dig a hole and put a bowl in the center.
Cover it with plastic held down by
stones. The next day, you'll see water in
the bowl. This happens because water
evaporates from the soil and condenses
on the plastic, running off into the bowl.

Monsoon

A monsoon is a seasonal wind that blows for about six months in one direction; then turns around and blows in the other direction for six months. In summer, moist winds from the ocean bring dark, rain-bearing clouds to the land. In winter, the cycle is reversed. Wind blows the air from the land to the sea, bringing cool, dry weather.

Dragon slayer
The ancient Hindus thought that a dragon stopped the monsoon from coming. The welcome rains would not appear until the dragon was killed by the god Indra.

Before the monsoon
During the early summer, the hot sun heats up the dry tropical land while the oceans stay cooler. As warm air rises above the land, cool, moist air from the sea rushes in to fill its place. The winds blowing the sea air bring heavy rainfall. This rainfall is the summer monsoon.

Life goes on
The rain is often so heavy that it washes away crops and floods the streets. Violent thunderstorms can also occur. But whatever the monsoon brings, life goes on.

Rice crops cannot grow on the parched land, so a monsoon is most welcome.

Where the wind blows

The monsoon is best known in Asia. But monsoon winds also bring rain to other places in the tropics, including Africa, South America, the southern United States, and Australia.

As the weather calms down, people reap the benefits of the monsoon.

The monsoon areas are colored red.

Monsoon in action

Monsoons are vital for agriculture. Once the monsoon begins, the wet conditions are ideal for farmers. They start plowing and planting young rice plants in the flooded fields.

After the rain

For six months, showers sweep across the land. Finally, the wind and rain die down. The cool air flows back toward the sea, and the land begins to dry.

41

A warm front

If weather forecasters say a "front" is on its way, then expect the weather to become wet and windy. A front is where a mass of warm, moist air bumps into a mass of colder, drier air, creating clouds and rain. Fronts move along with areas of low pressure, and the winds blow stronger as they pass by – like a speeding truck stirring up litter by the roadside.

Altocumulus clouds

Wisps of cirrus cloud

Curly warning
When you see wisps of feathery cirrus clouds in the sky, you can be sure a warm front is on its way.

Clouding over
After a while, the sky gets hazy and the clouds thicken. Fluffy altocumulus clouds appear, looking like balls of cotton. The wind grows stronger, making the sea very choppy.

Altostratus clouds

Nimbostratus clouds

Steady sheets of rain

The sea is very choppy.

Bumps point the same way the wind blows.

Hot line
On weather maps, a warm front is a line with red bumps on it.

Wet and windy
Soon the sky is dark with thick nimbostratus clouds. It begins to rain steadily and goes on raining for several hours. If it is cold enough, it may even snow.

43

A cold front

Fronts usually come in pairs. Often there is only a brief gap between one front passing and the next arriving. The first is a "warm" front because it brings warmer air. The second is a "cold" front and brings colder air and sometimes even stormier weather than the warm front.

Stratocumulus clouds bring occasional drizzle.

On the move
On a weather map, a cold front is a line with blue spikes. The spikes show which way the cold air is moving.

Brief relief
As the warm front moves away, the rain (or snow) stops and it gets warmer. Near the coast it stays cloudy, and there may be drizzling rain.

In summer inland, the sun comes out and it can get hot after the warm front has moved away.

Thundercloud

Storm overhead

You know the cold front is on its way when the wind becomes stronger, with gusts that rattle windows. The sky may fill with huge, dark thunderclouds that lash the countryside with rain or even hailstones.

Cumulus clouds

The sea is very rough.

Patches of blue sky appear.

It's all over

The worst of the storm is soon over. It feels colder as the clouds clear, leaving a blue sky with fluffy cumulus clouds – although there may still be more violent showers to come.

The sea is calmer.

Thunder and lightning

Hot, sticky summer days often end in violent thunderstorms. Dark, towering thunder-clouds send forks of lightning flashing across the sky, and booming thunderclaps fill the air. The electricity from just one bolt of lightning could light a small town for a whole year!

Holy thunder
Some American Indians believed that the sacred thunderbird made thunder by beating its enormous wings, and that lightning flashed from its beak.

Each fork of lightning is many lightning flashes running rapidly up and down the same path.

How near is it?
You can work out how far away a storm is by counting the seconds between a flash of lightning and a thunderclap. For every five seconds you count, the storm is one mile away.

Strike
Lightning always takes the quickest path to the ground, so tall trees and buildings are most likely to be struck. The world's tallest buildings are struck by lightning hundreds of times each year.

Thunder is the sound of air bursting as it is heated rapidly by lightning.

Lightning and thunder happen at the same time, but you see lightning first because light moves faster than sound.

Flash and crack

Inside a storm cloud, violent winds swirl snow, hailstones, and rain up and down. Electricity builds up in the cloud and escapes as a flash of lightning.

Lightning flashes between the bottom of the thundercloud and the ground.

Strange strikes

A park ranger was struck by lightning seven times, and survived! Over the years, he lost a toenail and his eyebrows, and his hair was set on fire twice.

Colors in the sky

The sky isn't always blue, even when it's nice out. Near sunset, it can be purple or red. This is because sunlight is made up of the seven colors of the rainbow, all jumbled together. As sunlight bounces in different ways off dust and other particles in the air, different colors appear.

Fishy bow
Australian aborigines worship a god who is half fish and half snake. He lives in holes in the ground. When he moves from one hole to another, he appears as a rainbow in the sky.

Rainbows are curved because of the way light hits the round raindrops.

Curving colors
When sunlight passes through raindrops in the air, the light splits into seven colors – red, orange, yellow, green, blue, indigo, and violet. Many raindrops help to create the pattern.

Make a rainbow

You can make your own rainbow with just a glass of water and bright sunlight. Stand the glass on white paper, facing the sun. The paper must be in shadow; the glass in bright sun. The sunlight will shine through the glass and split into the seven colors.

To see a rainbow, the sun must always be behind you.

Ring around the sun

When the sun shines through thin, icy cloud, a colored halo may appear. This is caused by ice crystals in the cloud splitting sunlight into the seven colors, just as raindrops do. But never look directly at the sun, as it will damage your eyes.

If there is a second bow, its colors are always the other way around.

You always see the colors in a rainbow in the same order, from red through to violet.

Changing weather

The world's weather has changed many times. About 10,000 years ago, great sheets of ice covered a third of the Earth. That was the last Ice Age. Today we live in a much warmer climate. Many scientists think we have harmed the atmosphere so much that the world is getting even warmer.

Giant elephants
In the last Ice Age, woolly mammoths, giant elephant-like animals, wandered the frozen land. Their long, hairy coats kept them warm in the icy winds.

Prehistoric weather
Millions of years ago, when dinosaurs roamed the land, much of Europe and North America was covered with forests. The climate was hotter and more humid than it is today.

Sun trap
Only a small portion of the sun's heat reaches the Earth. But the Earth stays warm because gases, such as carbon dioxide, trap the heat – just like the glass in a greenhouse. In the right amount, these gases keep the world nice and warm.

Carbon dioxide is made when we burn wood, coal, or oil. If we produce too much, the Earth may get too warm.

A big umbrella

When volcanoes erupt, they throw large amounts of dust and smoke high into the atmosphere. This cuts off sunlight, shading the ground like a big umbrella. If enough smoke and dust are produced, the Earth could get colder.

Some people believe that the last Ice Age was caused by a volcanic eruption.

In the Amazon rain forest, an area the size of Oregon is cut down every year for farming.

Save the trees

Trees take in carbon dioxide and release oxygen and moisture, which is turned into rain. Cutting down and burning trees may lead to less rainfall and the buildup of carbon dioxide. This could raise the Earth's temperature.

Tropical rain forests are vital in removing excess carbon dioxide from the air.

Pollution

You may find it hard to believe, but many things people do every day create pollution – which affects us today and in the future. Too much pollution can cause changes in the weather. It may get too hot in some places and cause floods or drought in others. Cutting down on pollution now means a cleaner world tomorrow!

Acid rain, carried by wind, can destroy pine forests thousands of miles away.

Pollution problems

Smoke and gases from factories pollute the air and may form smog. This is a mixture of smoke and fog that can make people sick. Car exhaust gives off poisonous gases that not only affect our lungs but can block out the sunlight.

Acid rain

Power stations that burn coal or oil to generate electricity release the waste gases into the air. The gases float with the wind until raindrops dissolve them, making "acid rain." This eats away at buildings and kills trees, plants, and life in rivers and lakes.

Test for acid rain

Here is an experiment you can try to test for acid in rainwater. You will need two finely chopped red cabbage leaves, distilled water (from a pharmacist), rainwater, a bowl, two glass jars, a measuring cup, and a sieve.

2 Strain the cabbage juice into a measuring cup. The liquid should be a dark purple color.

1 Put the leaves into the bowl. Get an adult to pour hot distilled water over them. Then let them stand for an hour.

3 Pour a few ounces of distilled water into one jar and an equal amount of rainwater, collected from your yard, into the other.

4 Add the same amount of cabbage juice to each jar. The water will change color. Compare the color of the distilled water (this stays the same) and the rainwater. If the rainwater turns red, it is acidic.

Rainwater

Distilled water

The stronger the acid, the redder the water gets.

The Earth's blanket

The ozone layer of our atmosphere protects us from the sun's harmful rays. But some spray cans that we use contain chemicals that can destroy it. Holes have appeared in the ozone layer, allowing some harmful rays to reach the Earth's surface. This could damage many living things.

The pink, purple, and black areas in this satellite photograph show the hole in the ozone layer over the Antarctic.

53

Weather lore

Nowadays, weather forecasters use satellites and radar to tell us what the weather holds. But before this, people used to look for clues in nature to predict the weather. They didn't just look at the skies – they also watched how animals, birds, plants, and insects acted. Some of the signs are reliable, but others aren't foolproof!

Frog-cast

One way to tell if it's going to rain soon is to look out for frogs. They love it when it's damp, and hate dry conditions. Since the air usually becomes humid before it rains, when you see more frogs around, you will know to expect rain soon.

Aches and pains

The weather affects the way we feel, so it's natural to expect that the way we feel can help predict the weather. Some people suffer aches and pains when damp, cold weather is on the way; others feel strange when thunder is near.

Red sky at night

People used to say a red sunrise meant bad weather to come, and a red sunset meant good weather to come. Try to watch the sky at sunrise and sunset to see if this saying is always correct.

Open and close
Pinecones are traditionally used to forecast the weather. Put a pinecone outdoors and watch what happens. It will open up in very dry weather and close up when it is damp.

The pinecone's scales open in dry weather.

Scales are tightly shut in wet weather.

Groundhog forecast
In the United States, people say that if you can see a groundhog's shadow at noon on the second of February, there will be six more weeks of winter. Fortunately, the groundhog isn't always right!

Flower power
When you want to know what the weather will be like, look out for the magic carpet flower. Its petals stay wide open in fine weather, but they close up when the sky grows dark.

Weather forecasting

To work out what weather is on the way, forecasters take measurements from weather stations all over the world. They also study photographs of the Earth taken from satellites in space. Then huge computers print out weather maps that show what the conditions are now and what they will be like in a few hours or a week from now.

The warm front is moving from right to left on this map, so the weather will stay good here longer than in the town. Fronts usually travel eastward, so move from left to right on weather maps.

Weather map

This picture shows some of the features you might see on a weather map, along with the kind of weather you might expect. Look for the warm front, which will bring stormy weather.

The weather is good here now, but it will turn for the worse as the warm front (bumpy red lines) moves in.

The barometer indicates changeable weather here. It will soon begin to drop, showing that a front is on its way, bringing rain.

Feathery cirrus clouds high up show that a front is on its way.

Mountaintops are often covered in clouds while valleys are clear. This is because the air high up is colder and can hold less water.

Stratus clouds

Air pressure is high here.

Isobars are lines drawn on the map to link up places where air pressure is the same. Isobars tell you where pressure is high and where it is low.

A change in the wind direction warns of a change in the weather.

The wind changes direction and gets stronger.

Nimbostratus clouds give steady rain.

Cirrostratus clouds

Altostratus clouds

A red line with bumps shows where a warm front touches the ground. It is moving from right to left.

The weather will improve for a while after the front has passed.

The day

During the course of each day, there are changes in the weather. On nice days, you can almost tell the time by the way the weather changes through the day – from the cool chill of dawn through the heat of the afternoon to the clear, calm evening.

Daily record
Why not make a note of the way the weather changes through the day ? You may learn to predict when the sun will come out or when it will rain.

Warm days and cool nights often bring morning mists.

Clouds are small and may fade away as quickly as they form.

Sunrise
Dawn is usually chilly because the ground loses heat steadily all night. It is often misty too, for the cool of the night makes water condense in the air.

Midday
As the sun climbs in the sky, morning mists fade away, and it gets warmer. By midday, a few fluffy cumulus clouds appear, made by rising warm, moist air.

Why is the sky blue?

Sunlight contains all the colors in the rainbow, but so mixed up that it seems white. The sky is blue because only blue light bounces off the gases in the sky. When we look at a blue sky, we simply see the blue part of sunlight reflected off the gases toward our eyes.

Toward sunset

As the sun drops lower toward sunset, its power to stir up the air gets weaker, so the end of the day is often calm and clear, with barely a cloud in the sky.

Mid-afternoon

Mid-afternoon is usually the warmest time of day. Often, however, the morning's fluffy cumulus clouds can build up and up until they interrupt the afternoon with brief but heavy showers of rain, or even thunderstorms.

Night

Once the sun has dropped below the horizon, it gets steadily colder – especially if there are no clouds to keep in the heat.

Index

*Sun
bather*

Mist

Snowflake

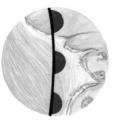

*Warm front on a
weather map*

Wind power

Rain-drop

Acknowledgments

**Dorling Kindersley
would like to thank:**
Simon Battensby for
photography on pages
16-17, 22-23, 28-29, 34-35,
42-43, 44-45.
Donks Models for models
on pages 16-17, 22-23,
28-29, 34-35, 42-43, 44-45.
Carl Gombrich, Gin von
Noorden and Kate
Raworth for editorial
assistance and research.
Sharon Grant for design
assistance.
Ron Lobeck for help with
writing text.
Jane Parker for the index.
Jim Sharp for help with
authenticating text.

Illustrations by:
John Bendall-Brunello,
Julia Cobbold, Louis
Mackay, Richard Ward.

Picture credits
t=top b=bottom c=center
l=left r=right
Frank Blackburn: 16tl.
Bracknell Weather Centre
24bl.
Bruce Coleman Ltd: 38br;
/Chris James 26b; /Kim
Taylor 20bl, 20bc, 20br; /
Roger Wilmshurst 24cr.
Frank Lane Picture
Agency: 32tl, 51t; /L.West
13tl, 25t.
R.K. Pilsbury: 13b, 24b.
Quadrant Picture Library:
36bl.
Science Photo Library: 5,
9br; /Martin Bond 54br; /
John Mead 12b; /NASA
53b; NCAR 18c; /
Nuridsany & Perennou
26t; /Dr.M. Read 51b.
Zefa: 39l, 47t; /K.L. Benser
19t; /Kalt 10bl, 10br,
11bl, 11br.